BRITISH TRAMS

Peter Waller

GLORY DAYS

Ian Allan PUBLISHING

Front Cover: Pictured in glorious sunshine at the Millhouses turning circle in Sheffield is No 265. This was one of a batch of 54 built in the Corporation's own workshops between 1936 and 1939, representing the last new trams bought by Sheffield before the outbreak of World War 2. Sister car No 264 now forms part of the collection of the National Tramway Museum at Crich. *J. Copland/Photobus*

Back cover: Built originally for service in London, 90 of the LPTB 'Feltham' class migrated to Yorkshire during the period from 1949 to 1951. Fifty were ex-Metropolitan Electric Tramways, such as No 525 illustrated here, with the remaining 40 being ex-London United Tramways. Two of the ex-MET cars, Nos 501 and 526, are preserved. *J. Copland/Photobus*

This page: Royal events were usually marked by the use of decorated trams and the last significant event during the first generation era was the Coronation of HM Queen Elizabeth II in 1953. One of the systems that recorded the event was Dundee and No 1, suitably decorated, is seen at Ninewells on 3 June 1953. *Michael H. Waller*

Contents

Previous page: The wheel turns full circle. Britain's first urban heritage tramway now serves Birkenhead, the location of Britain's first street tramway in 1860. Restored Birkenhead No 20 nears the Woodside terminus on 23 August 2001. *Richard Gillespie*

Acknowledgements

The author would like to thank the following for their assistance in putting together the illustrations for this book: C. Carter, Alistair Grieve, Peter Johnson, R. W. A. Jones (courtsey of the Online Transport Archive), Brian Morrison, Richard Gillespie, Arnold Richardson at Photobus, Neville Stead, and Ron White at Colour-Rail. A number of photographs were taken originally by close friends of the author's father, notably the late Bob Parr and the late Maurice O'Connor; the collections of these photographers are now held by the National Tramway Museum and the author is grateful to Glynn Wilton at the Museum for his assistance. Every effort has been made to identify all copyright holders. In the event that any errors have been made, please advise the author via the publishers so any corrections can be made in future editions.

First published 2003

ISBN 0 7110 2911 3

Published by Ian Allan Publishing

an imprint of Ian Allan Publishing Ltd, Hersham, Surrey KT12 4RG.
Printed by Ian Allan Printing Ltd, Hersham, Surrey KT12 4RG.

Code: 0303/B2

Morning Glory

The emergence of tramways was very much a consequence of the era in which they were developed. The British Isles witnessed a social and economic revolution during the 19th century. At the start of the century the country's population was predominantly based in the countryside; by the end of Victoria's reign the majority of people lived in town and cities. Over a period of 100 years the population had shifted from working primarily in agriculture to working in industry as Britain became the 'Workshop of the World'.

If there was one concept that could be regarded to have epitomised the Victorian age it was 'Progress', a belief that as society developed so also it improved. The epitome of this was perhaps the Great Exhibition of 1851. The 19th century witnessed a great swathe of social reforms – such as the various Factory Acts – and technical developments – such as improved sanitation, electricity, gas, telephones – which radically altered the lifestyle of many of the country's inhabitants. Progress, however, was not uniform and for many of the poorest life continued to be 'nasty, brutish and short'. Even as late as World War 1, the physical condition of the conscripts summoned to the defence of King and Empire was such as to give serious concern to the military authorities; indeed, for many of Kitchener's troops, the food provided by the army was far better in quantity and quality than they had been accustomed to at home.

The arrival of the streetcar, first introduced to Britain by an American in the 1860s, was but a further facet of this belief in progress. By the late 19th century no self-respecting town or city wanted to forego the privilege of possessing a tramway. For the citizens of Perth in the early 1890s, the local newspaper expressed a common sentiment:

'Perth is bestirring itself and the citizens seem determined that she shall no longer be known as "Sleepy Hollow". We have extended our water supply, we are going in for a pretty big scheme of street improvements, and the laying down of a tramway line between Perth and Scone is just on the eve of being carried into effect. From the report of the meeting of shareholders ... we are pleased to note that the designation of the company is the Perth and District Tramway's [sic] Company.... There cannot be the least doubt as to the benefit and public utility of a tramway system between two such places as Perth and Scone. The promoters of such a scheme are really public benefactors. The traffic between the two places has quite got beyond the control of the Scone Omnibus Company. This company has done good service in its day, but there is now room for a new and better way.' (*Perthshire Courier*, 20 June 1893)

Taken at Scone on 1 November 1905, the first day of electric trams in Perth, No 1 was recorded suitably bedecked for the occasion. The first trams in Perth had been 3ft 6in gauge horse trams belonging to the Perth & District Tramways Co, which had commenced operation on 17 September 1895, but these had been taken over by the corporation in October 1903 as a precursor to electrification. The electric trams, painted lake and cream, were to operate until 19 January 1929. No 1, built by Hurst Nelson, was one of 12 electric cars to operate over the small network.
Author's Collection

To many, it is the illuminated cars at Blackpool that epitomise the tradition of highly decorated trams. Based around toastrack car No 163, the 'Blackpool Belle' first made its appearance in 1959. It was to survive in service until 1978 when it was withdrawn; it was subsequently to be sold for preservation in the USA.
E. R. Hargreaves

Of all the 'Big City' operators in Great Britain, Birmingham was atypical in selecting the 3ft 6in gauge. This gauge was effectively the standard gauge for trams in the West Midlands and Black Country, but it made the trams an easy target when higher-capacity buses started to emerge. In 1929/30 Birmingham constructed two experimental cars, the first of which, No 842, built by Short Bros on English Electric 'Burnley'-style lightweight bogies, is shown when new. By this date, however, the tram was already under threat in Birmingham, with the conversion of the Bolton Road route to bus operation on 5 February 1930. Although this was not the first conversion in Birmingham – the Nechells route had succumbed to trolleybus operation in 1922 – it did represent the start of a gradual process of elimination which would have been concluded earlier had it not been for World War 2.
Ian Allan Library

A classic British double-deck tram, Gateshead No 61, is seen on the short section of interlaced track on Hill Street (near Gateshead East station) as it heads towards Newcastle Central station on one of the services that crossed over the Tyne. It was the presence of several low railway bridges in the town that was a factor in Gateshead operating a large fleet of single-deck trams.
R. W. A. Jones

5

Although he was ultimately eager to dispense with the city's trams during the 1930s and was even more reluctant to see them replaced by trolleybuses, Stuart Pilcher as General Manager in Manchester initially sought to improve the position of the tramcar through the construction of new four-wheel cars, such as No 263 illustrated here, between 1930 and 1932. When deemed surplus to requirements in Manchester, the cars were sold on to give further service in Aberdeen, Edinburgh, Leeds and Sunderland.
Ian Allan Library

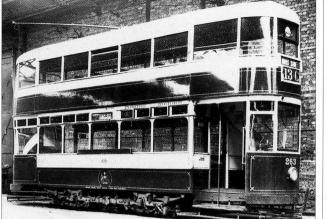

The last new first-generation electric tramway to open in the British Isles was that which replaced steam operation on the line between Swansea and Mumbles in 1928/29. By this date, however, some 20 electric systems had already been converted to bus or trolleybus operation in Britain, including those serving important towns like Ipswich and Wolverhampton. Two of the Swansea & Mumbles, trams head west towards Mumbles Pier in this view.
Neville Stead Collection

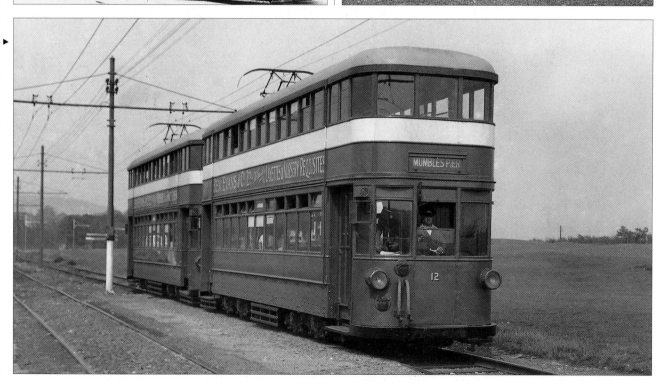

Introduction

It is now more than 140 years since the first pioneering tramway route opened and more than 130 years since the Tramways Act allowed for the widespread construction of tramways in the British Isles. In this period, the tram has gone from nowhere, through being the primary form of urban public transport and then being condemned as obsolete and outdated, to a new dawn where second-generation tramways are now perceived as being the means by which traffic congestion can be eased. For students of transport history there is a wonderful irony in this: one of the factors often cited by engineers and politicians seeking to abandon earlier tramways was that they caused, rather than solved, congestion.

When approaching the subject of the 'Glory Days' of Britain's tramways the fundamental question was – as with my earlier *Heyday of the Tram* – precisely when that period existed. Arguably, the period when the country's tramways were at their peak covered the first two decades of the 20th century when new systems opened on a regular basis. However, the period when the largest number of trams operated in the country occurred during the 1920s, but even by that date smaller systems – faced by the need to modernise and by the economic stagnation that occurred in the years immediately after the end of World War 1 – had already succumbed to the trolleybus or bus. In terms of the provision of a modern public transport service, it could be argued that the 1930s, when many of the major cities saw massive investment in tramways, could be seen as another candidate. Postwar, it is clear that as a functioning form of public transport, the tram was heading towards extinction and yet, with the growth of preservation, there were bright spots. Today, the country is witnessing a further period of expansion; however, it is unlikely that, given the costs of investment, the tram will ever have as universal a role as it had during the period before 1939.

In approaching the subject, this book does not pretend to be a detailed history of the British tramcar; other books have been published that provide a comprehensive history of individual systems or a more global account of the rise and fall of the British tram. Rather, it attempts through a series of chapters to examine popular attitudes to the tram and its development over more than 100 years.

It is possible to argue that there is a strong case for claiming that any decade from the start of the last century until the outbreak of World War 2 could be considered the true 'Glory Days'; for a younger generation, the arrival of new-generation tramways is perhaps more pertinent. Whatever the truth, it is clear that the tram has influenced, and will continue to influence, urban development for more than a century; it is this century that this book explores.

◄ Typical of the first-generation tramway in Britain is Sheffield No 161 recorded at the city's Midland station on 22 May 1949. A fully-enclosed four-wheel car, No 161 was built in the Corporation's own workshops on Peckham P22 trucks in 1933.
Michael H. Waller

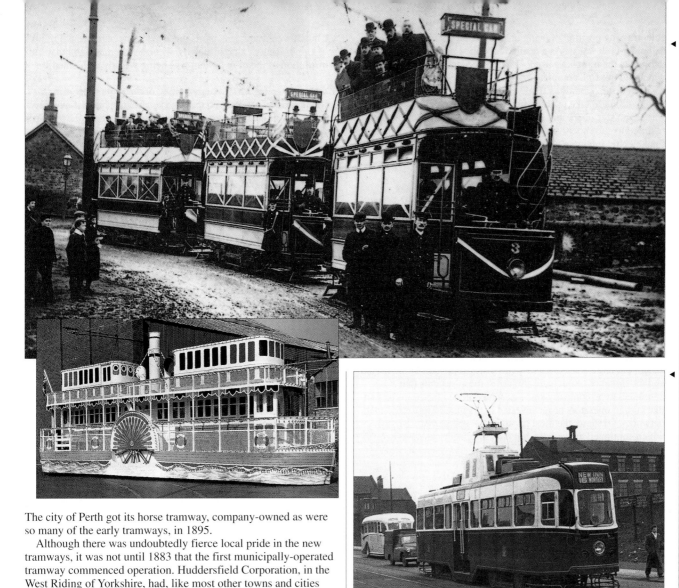

The city of Perth got its horse tramway, company-owned as were
so many of the early tramways, in 1895.

Although there was undoubtedly fierce local pride in the new
tramways, it was not until 1883 that the first municipally-operated
tramway commenced operation. Huddersfield Corporation, in the
West Riding of Yorkshire, had, like most other towns and cities
interested in the promotion of tramways, sought powers to
construct a network of lines in the borough. However, whilst
construction proceeded apace, the Corporation found itself in the

location of the city's Museum and Art Gallery – Cartwright Hall – opened in 1904), was also served by trams. Municipal munificence in Leeds did not stop with the purchase of Roundhay Park; the city fathers also acquired the Jacobean mansion of Temple Newsam with its extensive grounds. This too was served by trams; indeed, the York Road routes, of which Temple Newsam was one, survived to be the last routes operated in November 1959.

Apart from parks within the boundaries of the towns and cities of the Industrial Revolution, extensive estates, such as Temple Newsam, were acquired or given. One notable example of this was in 1906 when the Cadbury family donated an area of the Lickey Hills around Rednal to Birmingham. Access, at least in the era before the motorcar, was by bus as there was little incentive for a company, faced with losing its lease, to invest significantly in improvements to services along the Bristol Road. However, the corporation took over operation of the Bristol Road routes in 1911 and an extension to Rednal was completed on 14 April 1924, one of a number of developments that occurred on the Birmingham system during that period. Such was the scale of potential traffic over the route to Rednal that a loop was constructed at the terminus, being completed on 5 April 1925.

Apart from the creation of open public places, there was another revolution that would have an impact on the need for public transport – the growth of sport. It was during the late 19th century that the national obsession with spectator sport gradually developed as competitions and leagues gradually became formalised, particularly in terms of professional sports such as football and rugby league. The Football League was first established in 1888 and quickly expanded from the early years of the 20th century, with the creation of a second division, whilst the Northern Rugby Union – as the rugby league was then known – was created as a result of a breakaway in 1895. The factors behind the NRU were symptomatic of the strains between working class participants in sporting events, many of whom were expected to work six days a week and who were looking for compensation for loss of earnings, and the amateur establishment for whom any sort of compensation smacked of professionalism.

From the late 19th century onwards many of the great sporting venues that are still familiar names today were first developed with little more than basic facilities. But it was the early years of the 20th century that were to witness the golden age of stadium design and construction, with the name of Archibald Leitch to the fore. Bradford, for example, possessed three major sporting venues: Valley Parade, home of Bradford City from 1903, Odsal, home of Bradford Northern from 1934, and Park Avenue, home of Bradford PA from 1908 and also the location of the Yorkshire cricket

Another city that provided a dedicated siding for football fans was Leeds, where a spur ran into Low Fields Road adjacent to Leeds United's Elland Road ground. An unusual visitor to the siding on 24 October 1948 was 'Middleton Bogie' No 265, visiting the line during an LRTL tour of the system.
Michael H. Waller

One of a number of locations within the British Isles that catered for the holidaymaker in the era before package tours to the Mediterranean was Douglas, on the Isle of Man. Ferry services from England landed at Douglas Harbour, from where horse-drawn trams provided a service along the promenade. In this undated photograph, probably dating from the early years of the century judging from the fashions and the lack of cars, no fewer than three horse trams can be seen. Today it is still possible to ride on a horse-drawn tram from this location, although the view is now much different, with the horse tram route effectively curtailed to where the closest horse tram to the photographer can be seen and a replacement ferry terminal has been constructed.
LMSR/Ian Allan Library

The Hill of Howth tramway was Ireland's last traditional tramway. As with the Swansea & Mumbles line, this route provided access for city-dwellers to an area of natural beauty that drew countless visitors each year. Owned by the Great Northern Railway (Ireland) the line opened in two stages during 1901. A total of 11 trams were constructed to operate over the route, of which three – Nos 3, 8 and 7 – are pictured at Howth Summit. These three were amongst the original batch of eight delivered in 1901 by Brush for the opening of the line. Ownership of the line was to pass to CIE in 1958 and closure was to come on 31 May 1959. Sister cars Nos 2 and 4 were preserved as was No 3 for a period; it was broken up at the St James' Gate Brewery in Dublin during 1965. *R. W. A. Jones*

Recorded in Sutton depot, where the Hill of Howth fleet was based, this photograph gives a good impression of the nature of the facilities offered by an open-top double-deck tram. Whilst it must have been highly enjoyable to have made the trip around Howth on a good summer's day, the experience must have been considerably less pleasant in inclement weather. *R. W. A. Jones*

'TOURIST CAR – This car must be treated as a "special" car, and as such must, if necessary, give way to all "service" cars. Service cars, however, must assist as far as possible in ensuring a broken run for the Tourist Car. This Car is run with the object of giving visitors an opportunity of viewing Torquay as far as possible from the tram routes, and also of giving aged and invalids a comfortable ride extending over the period of time advertised.'

Other coastal resorts to operate tours include Scarborough, where a service operated for a few years prior to the outbreak of World War 1 and was reintroduced after the cessation of hostilities. In Southend, following the completion of the route along Southchurch Boulevard, a circular tour was introduced in the summer of 1914. Although the subject of debate, it seems likely that the circular continued to operate through the summers of World War 1 and into the 1920s. The appeal of the service, however, gradually declined during the 1920s and, despite attempts to reinvigorate it in the 1930s, the service ceased in July 1938 with the abandonment of the Boulevard route. Southport also

◀◀
Also pictured in Sutton depot is this view of the lower deck of Hill of Howth No 10. The seating, formed of central longitudinal seating, was unusual; the material, wood, was less so. Nos 9 and 10 were built by G. F. Milnes & Co and delivered to the line in 1902. No 10 was preserved after closure by the Tramway Museum Society and regauged to standard gauge. Now on display at the National Tramway Museum, it has also seen service in preservation on loan to Blackpool.
R. W. A. Jones

◀
Whilst not normally considered to be a seaside town, Sunderland's beaches could attract large numbers of day trippers. Two routes were built to serve Seaburn: one via Fulwell and one via Roker. The extension from Fulwell to Seaburn opened on 10 May 1937, the last of the system's prewar extensions, and here No 21 is pictured at the terminus. This tram was built in the Corporation's own workshops in 1933 using EMB Hornless trucks and was one of two that was constructed using the bodyshells of English Electric-built trams supplied to Mansfield & District in 1925. Note the stall offering hot water on the extreme left.
R. W. A. Jones

introduced a circular tour in 1913, which was developed in 1914 into the Grand Tour – 6.5 miles in length for the princely sum of 6d. The tour continued to operate during World War 1 and was supplemented in the early 1920s by a new Circular Tour. The Grand Tour last operated in 1924 and, with the contraction of the town's tramways the Circular Tour ran for the last time in 1932.

Apart from the systems that were to serve existing communities, there were also a number of tramways built aimed specifically at the holiday market. In Scotland, for example, there were two notable examples: the Cruden Bay line built by the Great North of Scotland Railway to link the hotel with the railway station and the Rothesay Tramways on the Isle of Bute. In Ireland, one of the pioneering electrified lines was the Giant's Causeway Tramway, which linked Portrush with the Causeway. On the Isle of Man, the Snaefell Mountain Railway was opened on 21 August 1895 to carry visitors to the top of the 2,100ft peak of Snaefell. In Wales, the much-mourned Llandudno & Colwyn Bay line provided a direct link between two of North Wales' most popular seaside resorts, whilst in Llandudno itself, the Great Orme Tramway opened in two stages, in 1902 and 1903, providing easy access to the summit. In South Wales, the world's oldest passenger railway, the Oystermouth, was also to become the last 'new' electric tramway to open – prior to more recent developments, however – when its fleet of massive double-deck trams was introduced on 2 March 1929. The most recent example of the tramway as tourist

service is perhaps that of Seaton, where a route has been constructed along the former Southern Railway branch line.

Alongside the special routes, many of the seaside operators provided unconventional trams to handle the traffic. Lytham St Annes bought 10 crossbench double-deck trams in 1905 and had 10 conventional trams converted to a similar style in 1906. Southport acquired its first toastrack single-deck tram in 1913 and eventually acquired six more between then and 1919. Southend obtained three crossbench single-deck trams in 1914 to be supplemented with a fourth in 1921. Rothesay possessed a range of toastracks and crossbench cars; it could claim to have both the largest toastracks in the country, with a seating capacity of 79, and the smallest – a converted four-wheel car with a capacity of 45. In Wales, the Llandudno & Colwyn Bay possessed four toastracks built in 1920.

However, it was in Blackpool that the tram designed to cater for the holidaymaker reached its zenith. Amongst the earliest trams to be delivered for the conduit tramway in 1885 were two open-top crossbench cars, whilst later deliveries to the Blackpool Electric Tramway Co Ltd prior to its take-over by the Corporation included the first of the famous 'Dreadnought' cars, with their double stairs at both ends and, for the time, enormous seating capacity of 86. With the Corporation's take-over, further 'Dreadnoughts' were acquired, including No 59, which is now preserved. Toastrack trams were first delivered in 1911 and between then and 1927

The second route to Seaburn, separated from that via Fulwell by a short distance at the coast, terminated in a loop. The route from Roker opened in May 1901 but was suspended during World War 2, and reintroduced, following the cessation of hostilities in Europe, on 4 June 1945. Pictured here awaiting departure back to Fawcett Street is No 38. This was one of six trams acquired second-hand from Manchester in 1937. Built originally in 1930 on Peckham P35 trucks in Manchester's own workshops, this car was originally No 503 in the Manchester fleet. The Seaburn via Roker route was to be converted to bus operation on 3 January 1954. The route to Seaburn via Fulwell was to survive to become Sunderland's last tram route, being converted to bus operation on 1 October 1954.
R. W. A. Jones

By the 1930s Blackpool's fleet of toastrack trams was ageing and, as part of Walter Luff's modernisation plan, 12 open-top single-deck trams were delivered from English Electric in 1934. Originally numbered 225-36, a handful remain in service almost 70 years after they were first built. No 231 is pictured when considerably newer, at Talbot Square on 16 April 1949.
Michael H. Waller

some 30 of the type were built. By the 1930s, when many of the original toastracks were life-expired, Blackpool took the opportunity of replacing them with a new generation of open-top tram, the 'Boat', of which 12 were built in 1934/35. Even when replacing the earlier generation of double-deck cars, the opportunity was taken to construct 12 of the replacement 'Balloon' cars as open toppers, although these were subsequently fitted with top covers during World War 2.

Today, Blackpool, Great Orme, Douglas and Snaefell are amongst the handful of survivors of the first golden age of British tramways. They continue to provide the service for which they were designed more than 100 years ago – carrying holidaymakers and day trippers in comfort.

Electric tramways promoted by the pre-Grouping railway companies were relatively rare; one notable example existed at Cruden Bay in northeast Scotland where the Great North of Scotland Railway operated a short 3ft 6in gauge tramway between the railway station and the railway-owned hotel. Opened in June 1899, the line was provided with two passenger trams, Nos 1 and 2, both of which were built in the GNoSR's workshops at Kittybrewster. Passenger services ceased on 30 October 1932, but the line remained open for the shipment of goods until it was suspended in March 1941 as a result of the war. Pictured in 1941 is No 2, by this stage in LNER livery. Both this car and No 1 were to survive (just), with the remains being used to recreate one preserved example.
W. A. Camwell/National Tramway Museum

One of the more anachronistic survivors amongst tramway of the British Isles is the horse tramway at Douglas. Although there were proposals early in the 20th century for the line's electrification, it was to remain horse-operated and, some eight decades after the last horse tramway in Great Britain disappeared, the horse-trams continue to ply their trade along Douglas's esplanade. On 18 September 2000, 1896-built (by Milnes) toastrack is recorded outside Derby Castle depot.
Peter Waller

In these secular days, when Sunday is now approaching the most important shopping day of the week, it is hard to imagine a society where the Sabbath was kept rigorously. In many towns and cities there was considerable opposition to the running of trams on Sunday and this commercial postcard purports to record the running of the first Sunday tram in the Nethergate, Dundee, on 10 September 1905. The reverse of the card, postmarked 27 September 1905 (at 8.45pm!), bears the message 'This is the Sunday car for you, Mary, and I hope you may enjoy many a run on them'. No 32 was one of a batch of 20 trams delivered as open-toppers by the Electric Railway & Tramway Carriage Co. *Author's Collection*

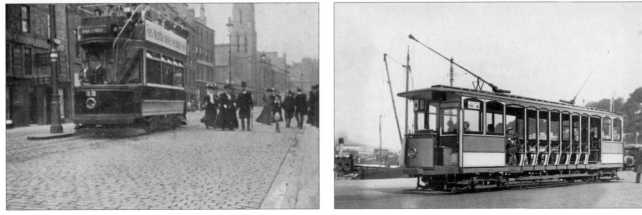

For more than 30 years the Isle of Bute could lay claim to be one of Britain's most isolated electric tramways – the 3ft 6in gauge system of the Rothesay Tramways Co. Opened on 19 August 1902 to replace a 4ft 0in gauge horse tramway, the system was largely designed to cater for holidaymakers. This scene illustrates, closest to the camera, car No 8, one of 10 crossbench trams manufactured by the Electric Railway & Tramway Carriage Works of Preston in 1902 for the opening of the system, with two further trams visible in the background. The date is circa 1910. *Author's Collection*

Recorded towards the end of its life, on 16 August 1936, Rothesay No 19 was one of five crossbench cars delivered by Brush in 1903. In 1931 the Rothesay livery changed from the red and white of the previous photograph to blue and cream. Although the tram looks in excellent condition, the system has barely a month to go, being abandoned on 30 September 1936. *Maurice J. O'Connor/ National Tramway Museum*

The Great Orme is more properly regarded as being formed of two funiculars, but to the majority of its passengers it had all the appearance of a traditional tramway, with overhead and trolleypoles. Recorded on 31 July 1976, during the glorious summer of that year, No 5 ascends near the passing place on the lower section, with Llandudno Bay forming a dramatic backdrop.
P. H. Groom

20

Escape from the Elements

In July 1839, giving evidence to a Parliamentary Committee, Charles Saunders of the Great Western Railway, when asked about the conveyance of third-class passengers, commented that the GWR would arrange to convey 'the very lowest orders of passengers' one day, but that no decision had been taken. He continued that were such passengers to be carried, it would probably be once a day, at very slow speed in carriages of an inferior description at a very low price, perhaps at night. Fortunately for the GWR's intending passengers, Parliament passed the Railways Act eventually which required all railway companies to provide a basic service – the so-called 'Parliamentary' train – of a reasonable standard.

With the dawn of the tramway age the promoters seem to have reverted to the GWR's attitude towards the travelling public. The first horse trams were relatively small, designed for haulage by either one or two horses. Both single- and double-deck horse-drawn trams existed; the former tended to provide covered passenger accommodation, but with open platforms, as for much of the tramway era, the members of the crew were provided with

little or no protection from the elements. Double-deck horse trams tended to be open-topped. It was only with the appearance of steam trams that double-deck trams were provided with enclosed top decks in order to protect the passengers from the smoke and steam of the engine. For the crews, however, there remained no protection. *The Yorkshire Post* of 25 October 1877 reported on an early trial of the use of a steam-hauled tram in Leeds. For the purposes of the trial, a standard horse-trailer was used:

> 'Altogether the trial passed off very satisfactorily with the exception of the discomfort caused to outside passengers by the emission of fumes and grit from the funnel; but we understand that can easily be obviated. The funnel, however, sends forth no smoke, and there need be no steam. The motion of the car is almost noiseless, and few horses passed on the road appeared to be disturbed by its appearance.'

Despite the optimism of the local paper, no doubt reflecting the positive views of the promoters of steam trams, the actuality was

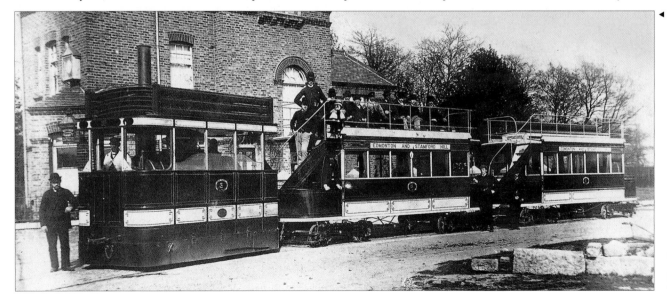

◄ Pictured outside the offices of the North London Tramways Co is Merryweather-built locomotive No 3 and trailer cars Nos 8 and 2. The route between Stamford Hill and Ponders End was originally opened as a horse tramway in 1881 and converted to steam-tram operation four years later. The passengers on the open upper-decks would have had little protection from the smoke and steam from the engine.
Ian Allan Library

Pictured outside Lime Street station in Liverpool can be seen four of the corporation's fleet of top-covered electric trams. Of the quartet, three are shown with the Bellamy top-cover whilst the third possesses a full-length roof but open balconies.
Ian Allan Library

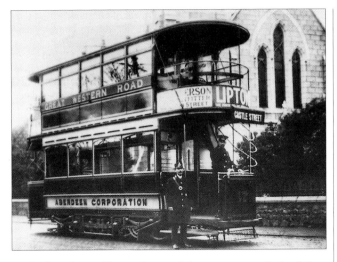

◄◄ Exemplifying a double-deck car fitted with full-length roof but retaining open balconies and vestibules is Aberdeen No 17 pictured during World War 1. This was one of a batch of 12 cars delivered by Brush in 1901; top covers were fitted from 1904 onwards. *Author's collection*

◄ Pictured in June 1949, Aberdeen No 76 exemplifies the double-deck tram fitted with top cover and enclosed vestibules, but still retaining open upper-deck balconies. No 76 was one of a batch of six built by the local manufacturer J. T. Clark in 1912/13 and was fitted with an extended top cover from new. The lower-deck vestibules were enclosed on all six cars during 1923 and 1924. *Michael H. Waller*

The first phase of improving conditions was generally the fitting of top covers to existing open-top trams. In Bradford, the passengers were noted, almost from the start of the electric trams, boycotting the open top-deck in adverse weather conditions; after all, for passengers who had got used to covered tops with the steam trams, the open electric cars represented a retrogressive step. The Liverpool manager until his untimely death aged 49 in 1905, Charles Revill Bellamy, was a pioneer of providing covered top-deck accommodation. The so-called 'Bellamy' roof first appeared in 1902. The initial design was for a wooden-framed structure inserted within the upper-deck railings and fitted with canvas blinds rather than glass; in good weather the canvas was rolled up. However good this was in theory, in practice the canvas proved less than efficient as Bradford discovered when it ordered six 'Bellamy'-type top covers from G. F. Milnes & Co following inspection of the Liverpool examples in 1902. In the short period that one of the canvas-fitted cars was running, it was reported that a cart horse was caused to panic resulting in a cartload of mineral water being deposited on the road surface. It soon became the norm for 'Bellamy'-type tops to be fully glazed throughout. Individual operators also experimented with their own design of top-cover; in Bradford, for example, the Thornbury Works' foreman, Arthur Bailey, designed his own form of top cover, known as the 'Bailey' top, in 1903 and these were soon fitted to a large proportion of the fleet. One of the most important aspects of British tramcar design was that trams could be and often were

significantly modified during their operational career with the latest design developments.

The early types of top cover merely enclosed the seating accommodation on the upper decks; the balcony and stairs remained uncovered and, particularly in bad weather, the stairs must have been treacherous. The next phase of tramcar development was to see the balconies provided with covers. Cars of this type started to appear towards the end of the first decade of the 20th century, although progress was by no means universal – it was not until 1912 that the first trams in Liverpool, for example, were fitted with covered balconies. As early as 1904, Dick Kerr exhibited new a tram with covered top and balconies for display at the Tramway & Light Railway Exhibition in London. As systems continued to expand, so their need for new trams was perpetuated and operators were able to improve the specifications for new deliveries. For example, in October 1903, Leeds sought tenders for a batch of 25 open-top trams; however, in January 1904, the companies from whom tenders had been sought were advised that the specification was now altered to include a top cover. In the event, Brush won the contract and the 25 cars were delivered between July and November 1904.

Whilst the passengers on the top deck were gradually being offered better conditions, the drivers remained in the open. The next phase of tramcar development was to see the lower deck vestibules fully enclosed. The first cars to be so treated appeared in the years before the outbreak of World War 1 and the process

Across the Pennines, another 4ft 0in gauge system was not so hampered by MoT restrictions. Blackburn was permitted to operate fully-enclosed trams on its network and typical of the fleet towards the end of its life is No 41, seen at the station on 18 April 1949. This was one of a batch delivered from Milnes in 1900 which were originally open-top but, with a small number of exceptions that remained open-top throughout their careers, all were rebuilt. By this date the system, as is evident from the condition of the tram, was increasingly careworn; indeed, at the date of the photograph, the system had less than five months to go. The last two routes – towards Darwen and towards Intack were converted to bus operation on 2 July 1949 and 3 September 1949 respectively.
Michael H. Waller

By the mid-1930s, Glasgow was faced by increased pressure on its existing tramcar fleet and, as a result, constructed two prototype cars, Nos 1141 and 1142, in 1936/37. These were the first trams delivered to Glasgow that featured segregated cabs a style which set the pattern for all new trams constructed for Glasgow thereafter. No 1141 is recorded near Coplawhill on 10 August 1952 whilst running on track normally used only by the PWD.
Michael H. Waller

change came, however, 20 years later when, between 1930 and 1931 all 10 were rebuilt as fully-enclosed four-wheel cars. It is open to debate precisely how much of the original cars survived the rebuilding exercise – it was quite common practice in tramway circles to class a completely new car as a rebuild to avoid having to obtain authorisation (indeed some of the original Blackpool 'Standard' cars were notionally rebuilds of the earlier 'Motherwell' cars) – but in terms of composition of the fleet the 10 were always regarded as having been built in 1900. The prudence that this represented at the time was perhaps short-sighted as, when the tramways came under threat in the mid-1950s, it was the average age of the fleet that counted much against the survival of the Dundee fleet.

In the development of the standard double-deck enclosed tram, there were often local circumstances that meant that not every stage could be fulfilled. In the case of Bradford, for example, with its 4ft 0in gauge trams, the Ministry of Transport, concerned by the gradients on hills and the potential for trams to be blown over, restricted the Corporation to operating only open-balcony double-deck cars.

By the mid-1920s, the standard enclosed double-deck tram had been developed and ensured that both passengers and crew were now able to travel in vehicles that offered full protection from the

climate. For the driver, however, these traditional trams still required them to stand for long shifts at the controls. It would be the next generation of trams that would start to provide drivers with segregated cabs and seats.

The turning point in terms of the improved conditions for the driver came, for the most part, in the early 1930s when many of the larger fleets were either continuing to expand or were looking to replace older types. In Glasgow, for example, the last traditional double-deck trams were the so-called 'Kilmarnock Bogies' constructed between 1927 and 1929. Thereafter, for the next few years, the Corporation's workshops were fully engaged in the rebuilding of the 'Standard' cars as fully enclosed, but come the mid-1930s there was a need for more trams as the normal requirements had increased by about 100 trams per day, to just under 1,000. In 1936/37 two experimental saloon bogie cars, Nos 1141 and 1142, were constructed. These cars were the first in Glasgow to be fitted with segregated drivers' cabs and seats and were the forerunners of the highly successful 'Coronation' and 'Cunarder' cars built between 1937 and 1954.

In London, although the London County Council had persisted with traditional style double-deck cars – exemplified by the 'HR/2'

class of trams constructed in 1930 and 1931 – London United Tramways and Metropolitan Electric Tramways, prior to the take-over by the LPTB in 1933, jointly produced the 'Feltham' bogie car. The production batch of cars was based around three prototypes – Nos 320 (of April 1929), 330 (of October 1930) and 331 (of June 1930 – now preserved). The first of these was fitted with separate drivers' cabs and with seats and this set the pattern for the 100 production 'Feltham' trams produced from December 1930 onwards.

Not all major operators, however, took the opportunity to provide better conditions for the crew when modernising their fleets in the period. Perhaps the most notable exception to this policy was in Liverpool, where the General Manager W. G. Marks was normally a major proponent of the latest in tramway technology. Whilst he may have been at the forefront of the adoption of tramway reservations, in terms of the modern tramcars he designed for the system – most notably the 'Green Goddesses' and the 'Baby Grands' – the results were highly conventional in that the drivers continued to stand on the unsegregated platforms provided.

It was not only the major operators that sought to invest in improved tramcar design in the 1920s and 1930s. In 1926, for example, Bradford sought to escape the straightjacket imposed by

the Ministry of Transport and constructed an advanced single-deck tram, No 1, which was fitted with separate cabs and drivers' seats. It was, unfortunately, not an experiment perpetuated with as the seating capacity, at 34, was considered too low. A decade later, South Shields, to cite a second example, constructed a one-off streamlined tram, No 52, which was built by English Electric. Again fitted with segregated cabs and drivers' seats, the car was another to have a relatively short career in its home town, being sold to Sunderland in 1946.

Of all British operators, it was perhaps Blackpool that came closest, at this stage, to operating a fully segregated fleet. During the 1930s, under the management of Walter Luff, who had been appointed in 1933 at a time when the position of the trams in the town was by no means secure, a fleet of modern streamlined trams was built. The origins of this programme dated to a report Luff presented to the Council on 20 February 1933 in which he advocated a five-year plan for the development of the tramway. Central to this policy was the purchase of new trams and, in furtherance of this, he unveiled a brand-new tram produced following consultations by English Electric. This new tram, No 200, was officially launched in June 1933 and, following the adoption of Luff's strategy, a further 83 trams were delivered by English Electric between then and 1935. These trams comprised four distinct models: the fully enclosed single-deck railcoaches, the open-top single-deck 'Boats', the fully-enclosed double-deck 'Balloons', and the open-top double-deckers. These 84 new cars were supplemented by two further batches of trams before the

outbreak of World War 2. From Brush in 1937 came 20 single-deck railcoaches similar in style to the earlier English Electric models whilst, in 1939, 12 trams were delivered from English Electric. These cars, Nos 10-21, were known as 'Sun Saloons', as a result of their half-height windows and canvas roofs, but were found to be unpopular in service when operating in bad weather, earning themselves the nickname of 'Cattle Trucks'. The 12 were soon fitted with permanent roofs. However, the result of Luff's policy was that by the outbreak of World War 2, Blackpool possessed a fleet of which the vast majority was less than a decade old; it was a fleet profile that was to stand Blackpool in good stead in the decades after World War 2 when the remaining urban fleets in Britain were rapidly disappearing. Perhaps the ultimate tribute to Luff's foresight comes with the fact that, some 60 years after the first of the type was introduced, a number of the trams supplied in the 1930s are still in service, either recognisably or as the basis of more modern rebuilds.

Whilst places like Blackpool and Glasgow did improve conditions for both passengers and drivers, and most operators who survived into the 1930s did improve conditions for passengers, it's certainly true to say that for most tramway systems the crews would have welcomed the demise of the tram. The classic film *The Elephant Will Never Forget* perhaps summarises the position very well: 'And what was the Tram Driver thinking – that man who stood with his back to us and whose face we probably never saw... Oh well, in thirty-six hours he'll be a bus driver, and for the first time in forty-two years he'll be sitting down...'

Although Marks was generally a progressive manager at Liverpool, particularly in terms of his modernisation and expansion of the infrastructure, when it came to tramcar design, however, he was less up-to-date. In the construction of both the 'Baby Grands' and 'Green Goddesses' he retained the traditional pattern of the platform, with the driver standing unsegregated. Pictured at the Pierhead on 24 July 1949 is 'Green Goddess' No 185. This was one of the 1937-built batch fitted with EMB Lightweight bogies. *Michael H. Waller*

Stockport was one of the 'small town' systems that bucked the trend in the 1930s and survived into the postwar years. A small system, centred on the complex junctions of Mersey Square in the town centre, Stockport operated joint services with neighbouring Manchester and with the SHMD Board. Although not acquiring new trams during the 1930s, Stockport continued to rebuild its existing fleet; indeed when it fitted a top cover to No 13 in 1944 it was the last tram in Britain to be so treated. The penultimate Stockport car to be fitted with a top cover, and thus the penultimate in Britain was No 1, which had been originally delivered by the Electric Railway & Tramway Wagon Co in 1901. No 1 was fitted with its top cover in 1941 and was renumbered 30 in 1944. In its later guise, No 30 is pictured in Mersey Square on 14 May 1949. By this date the Stockport system was gradually being abandoned; the town's last trams operated on 25 August 1951. *Michael H. Waller*

Evening Shadow

Enthusiast interest in tramways seems to have been much later to develop than that in railways. Whilst the Stephenson Locomotive Society may have been founded in 1909, it was only as the threat to the future of the tramcar became ever more obvious that the Light Railway Transport League was founded in 1937, primarily as a campaigning group for the retention and development of trams – 'Advocating Tramway Development' as the sub-title for the League's journal *The Modern Tramway* described it. The early years of the LRTL were not wholly happy, with a split occurring between it and the new Tramway & Light Railway Society and as a result of the exigencies of the wartime years.

Apart from the publication of *The Modern Tramway* the LRTL also acted as a forum through which enthusiasts could meet – there were numerous local area groups that met on a regular basis with times and locations advertised in advance in the magazine – and as an organiser of tours and visits. Again these were promoted through the pages of *The Modern Tramway*. Inevitably, activities were curtailed by the war, both in terms of accessibility and by the fact that many of the League's members were serving in the forces, but even during the war it was possible to organise events, as this announcement in the March 1945 issue of *The Modern Tramway* made clear:

'8th April (1945) – Depot visit for members in Southampton and District. Meet at Central Station tram stop at 12.15 noon [sic] for visit to Shirley and Portswood depots, by kind permission of Southampton Corporation Transport. In view of the large increase in membership in this area of late, it is thought that this repeat visit will be appreciated, and a good attendance is looked for.'

By the late 1940s many of Britain's first generation tramways could present a depressing sight to enthusiasts. Pictured awaiting its final fate is Southampton No 43 at Shirley Depot on 8 January 1949. Originally delivered from Hurst Nelson in 1903 as part of a batch of 10, No 43 was one of a quartet to be rebuilt in 1906/07 with the remainder being so treated between 1921 and 1929. Despite the rebuild, No 43 and the rest of the batch remained in the open-top condition throughout their working lives. Two were withdrawn in the late 1920s, but the remaining eight were retained until final withdrawal in 1948. It was seeing the condition of the trams awaiting scrapping that encouraged the LRTL to purchase No 45 for preservation in 1948, thereby starting the process that led ultimately to the creation of the National Tramway Museum at Crich.
Michael H. Waller

The opportunity was taken during the LRTL Convention of May 1950 to run a tour over the Sunderland system using No 26. This car, built in Sunderland's own workshops in 1935, was the first of three constructed that year on EMB Hornless trucks. The three represented the first Sunderland trams to be fitted with glass roof lights. The special, run on 28 May 1950, is seen here at the Seaburn, via Roker, terminus.
Michael H. Waller

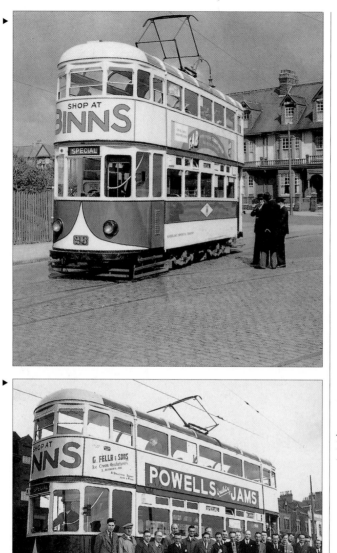

One of the rituals during the course of any special was the group photograph, and the special run in connection with the LRTL Convention in May 1950 was no exception. In all, some 40 members of the LRTL attended the Convention, at which, inter alia, it was decided to hold the following year's Convention at Edinburgh rather than on the Isle of Man. Here the passengers on the special are pictured in front of No 26.
Author's Collection

It was also normal practice after the event for the magazine to provide a full report of the day's activities. Thus the May 1945 issue of *The Modern Tramway* carried the following report:

'Southampton Depot Visit

'A large party of local members, together with members of the Southampton Tramcar Passengers' Association, visited Southampton tramway depots on 8th April. Mr. A. G. Barnes, Chief Inspector, S.C.T., met the party at Central Station car stop, and car no. 107 (newly painted) was boarded, the first port of call being the Floating Bridge, where the S.C.T.'s "marine division" was sampled. ... On the return to *terra firma*, the tram was again boarded and ran to Shirley Depot, where numerous types of tram were brought out for photography, including No. 81, which was just out of the paint shop. A further tram journey took the party to Portswood where this second depot was inspected and tea later taken in the comfortable Staff Canteen. The repair shops were also visited, No. 10 being seen with truck dismantled for overhaul, and other cars awaiting repairs.

'A hearty vote of thanks was accorded to Mr. Barnes, and to the General Manager, for the facilities accorded, and members dispersed after travelling back to the Central Station.'

It was during one of these tours to Southampton that the first tramcar to be preserved in Britain – No 45 – was identified and purchased following an eventful tour organised over the network on 29 August 1948. The postwar condition of many of Britain's tramways, a contributory factor no doubt to their gradual demise, was apparent during this tour of Southampton. Using car No 37, the tour initially suffered a broken trolleyhead, which required attention from the breakdown tender, before being derailed at the junction of the Shirley and Millbrook routes. The proposed purchase and its financial implications were recorded in *The Modern Tramway*:

'It has been suggested that the League should in similar fashion [to North American practice] purchase one of the remaining knife-board-type open-top cars of Southampton Corporation, before the last examples are disposed of. We have now investigated the possibility, and have pleasure in announcing that Leeds City Transport Department have kindly agreed to store the car for us in one of their depots, and to allow it to be operated occasionally over their tracks. Southampton Corporation Transport Department have agreed to let us have one of the remaining knife-board cars, complete and in running order, for the sum of ten pounds.

'The successful carrying out of this project will depend upon the support of those of our members who are interested in thus preserving one of the last remaining standard-gauge open-top cars in the country. The cost of transporting the car from Southampton to its new home in Leeds is expected to amount to at least £40, and we appeal to our historically-minded members to subscribe liberally towards this fund.'

Although the funds were to be raised to secure No 45, this early experience in preservation was to bring two important lessons: firstly, that the purchase price was but part of the story and, secondly, the fundamental problem of housing tramcars in an age before the creation of the museum at Crich. The next decade was to witness the purchase or promise of numerous cars for preservation, some of which were declined and others of which only received a temporary reprieve from the scrapyard before the lack of secure accommodation rendered them vulnerable.

The plight of these first preserved trams was highlighted by the career of No 45 in its early years in private ownership. The tram was initially sent to Leeds, where it was an unwelcome visitor to Kirkstall Depot. The unpopularity of this 'guest' was highlighted in a local paper report, in May 1949, recording the tram's transfer

◄ For delegates to the 1950 LRTL Convention, when business and other activities permitted, there was the opportunity to sample the other tramway delights that Sunderland could offer. One of the system's notable features was the number of second-hand trams in service – with examples coming from Ilford (via the LPTB), Accrington, Huddersfield, Manchester, Portsmouth, South Shields and Bury. Perhaps the most famous of all the system's second-hand purchases was No 100, the prototype 'Feltham' delivered to the Metropolitan Electric Tramways (as No 331) in 1930 and renumbered 2168 by the LPTB in 1933. This car, acquired in 1937, was recorded at Seaburn during the Convention. After its withdrawal the following year, it passed into preservation and can be seen at the National Tramway Museum. *Michael H. Waller*

◄ Pictured at Swan Inn, the junction of the Belle Isle and Hunslet routes, during the course of an LRTL tour on 24 October 1948 is 'Middleton Bogie' No 265. Standing prominently by the door is the late Bob Parr, well known as a tramway photographer, who at the time was the LRTL's Leeds Area Representative. *Michael H. Waller*

LRTL tours were often organised postwar in order to mark the demise of an operator or route; less common were tours that marked more positive developments. One of the latter, however, occurred in Sheffield on 22 May 1949 when the visiting LRTL members were able to travel over the city's extensive tramway network on board the then unique No 501, which had entered less than three years earlier. Although this was destined to be the last car built in the corporation's own workshops, it was to be the basis for a batch of 35 new trams delivered between 1950 and 1952, built by Roberts of Horbury. No 501 is pictured at Midland station during the tour. *Michael H. Waller*

Another group photograph, but, this time in slightly less happy circumstances: towards the end of Leeds' system in 1959 a tour party stands in front of one the surviving 'Felthams' at the Temple Newsam terminus. The size of the tour party necessitated the use of two vehicles, and the second car can be seen behind the Feltham. *Photobus*

to Blackpool (where it was to remain for more than eight years before being sent back to Hampshire for display at Lord Montagu's museum at Beaulieu before, once again, heading north to secure accommodation at Crich):

'This old warrior left Leeds unwept, unhonoured and unsung
'Without fuss – nobody saw it off – the 1902 tram that Leeds didn't want left Kirkstall-road tram depot to-day on a trailer for Blackpool...

'For five months it had been in the Leeds depot. Its departure was as chilly as its reception – it trundled down the Guiseley road, down into Wharfedale – with a foot to spare at Burley railway bridge – and on, past Addingham and Ilkley, to Skipton.

'When it reached Gisburn scores of sleepy housewives rubbed their eyes in surprise at the sight of a tram in a country lane.

'So Leeds rid itself of a museum-piece, bought by the Light Railway Transport League, from Southampton Corporation for £10, and sent to Leeds by mistake.

'Resting place
The Transport Committee announced: "We have no intention of setting up a tramcar museum in Leeds. We don't want this car."

'Finally it was decided to garage the tram in Leeds until a permanent home could be found, and Blackpool Transport Department eventually agreed to have it.

'Mr J. W. Fowler, chairman of the Executive Council of the Light Railway Transport League added a last word to-day: "We are very pleased that it has been found what might be called a last resting-place"

Other tramcars preserved in the early days of the LRTL's Museum Committee also came to find homes in unusual places. Sunderland No 100, formerly MET No 331 and the prototype 'Feltham' car, was to be found stored in Bradford Corporation's Thornbury works for many years, the first standard gauge tram in the city since the demise of the dual-gauge through service with Leeds during World War 1 and the last until the ill-fated West Yorkshire Transport Museum project. Newcastle No 102 was another to find itself stored at the Montagu museum at Beaulieu, whilst ex-London No 1858 was displayed for many years at Chessington Zoo before its transfer to the East Anglian Transport Museum at Carlton Colville.

Not all of these early preserved trams, however, led such a charmed life. Amongst the casualties were two Liverpool trams preserved in the early 1950s, including 1911-built No 558, that

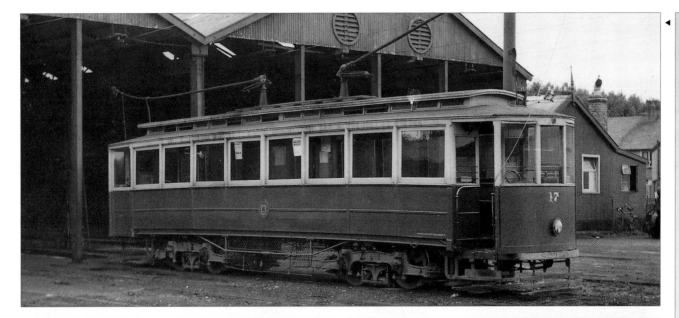

were scrapped after vandalism and three Dublin trams – 'Standard' No 129, 'Luxury' No 132 and 'Dalkey Bogie' No 328 – that were saved after the closure of the Dublin system in 1949 but were again to be scrapped after vandalism. Another casualty was Aberdeen No 73, acquired by the Scottish Tramway Museum Society, but again scrapped for want of a permanent home. Efforts

In its later days, the mainstay of the L&CBER operation was provided by 10 open-top trams bought from Bournemouth Corporation in 1936. Built originally in the early 1920s by Brush as Bournemouth No 128, No 12 is seen on less than an ideal day for those passengers sitting on the top deck as it heads westwards towards Llandudno. The line closed on 24 March 1956 and one of the 10 ex-Bournemouth cars, No 6 (ex-Bournemouth No 85 dating from 1914), was to be preserved. More recently the body of a similar car to No 6 has been acquired and moved to North Wales as part of a scheme to reopen part of the line. *Ian Allan Library*

to preserve one of the ex-Manchester 'Pilcher' cars from Aberdeen also failed, whilst an offer of two Dundee cars, including one of the 'Lochee' cars, was rejected by the LRTL Museum Committee on the grounds of the lack of storage. Dundee Corporation had offered them free of charge provided an immediate move could be organised. The then curator of Dundee's local museum commented that he'd have accepted one for the Albert Square museum but that it was impossible to get in.

In the late 1940s, however, the necessity of securing a representative selection of tramcars for preservation was still perceived to be unlikely as many operators were still considered to have a long-term future. As the 1950s marched on, however, it became clear both that the days of the trams were numbered and that it was essential to secure a permanent site for display. That there is a representative selection of British tramways for future generations to enjoy ultimately comes down to the fact that a number of significant operators, most notably Leeds, Glasgow and Sheffield, survived to the end and ultimately proved co-operative to enthusiasts and, secondly, to the fact that by the end of the 1950s the Tramway Museum Society had identified a site at Crich in Derbyshire for the creation of a museum.

If, however, the number of trams preserved at the time had been the sum of the national collection, then the history of Britain's tramways would have been relatively ill-served. However, it has been possible over the past 40 years to extend the range of trams preserved through the acquisition and restoration of many older trams that had been sold off for reuse as sheds or cottages.

The first tram to be restored from a near derelict condition was Bradford No 104. When Bradford's system closed in May 1950, efforts were made to persuade the Manager to retain No 51, the official last tram, but these fell on deaf ears. However, there were proposals from a representative of Bradford Northern Rugby League FC to take a complete car, No 104, for display at Odsal stadium. Due to a mix up, these plans seemed to have gone sadly awry when the body, divested of its truck and electrical equipment, was sent to Baildon Moor for conversion into a cottage. Following discussions, the Baildon family received the lower deck of another tram and No 104 was transferred to Odsal where it became a scoreboard. Its sojourn in the open was, however, to be short and it returned to Thornbury Works in mid-1953 for restoration. The reconstruction of the tram was a long process, requiring the acquisition of a truck from Sheffield, a trolleybase from Liverpool and myriad other parts from the Corporation's own stores or from individuals. The work was completed in July 1958 and the fully restored tram was able to travel over the still extant track at Thornbury Works for the first time under its own power for more than eight years on 21 July 1958. For the next five years the tram made regular appearances running over the Thornbury tracks until power supply problems forced these to be stopped. It last ran in 1966 but remained at Thornbury Works until transfer to Bradford's Industrial Museum in the mid-1970s.

In the half century since No 104 was rescued for restoration, the number of trams undergoing similar treatment has increased phenomenally. At the National Tramway Museum, for example, the availability of tramcar bodies has resulted in the restoration of a steam-tram trailer from Dundee, Leicester No 76, Manchester No 765 (now at Heaton Park), Stockport No 7, LCC No 106, Sheffield No 74, London 'E1' class No 1622 and others; each of these trams fills a perceived gap in the museum's overall collection and thus helps to tell the full story of the tramcar in Britain. And Crich is not alone in rebuilding trams for future generations: at Beamish, Heaton Park, Summerlee, Birkenhead and in other museums across the country examples of long-lost trams are being reborn and, provided the funding continues (because these restoration projects are not cheap), further examples will emerge.

It is doubtful whether, when No 45 was first acquired and the LRTL Museum Committee first established, those involved ever perceived the fact that the number of preserved or vintage trams in Britain would exceed modern trams in public service, but that is what has occurred – a truly remarkable achievement.

One of a number of trams to lead a somewhat itinerant life during their early days in preservation, London 'HR/2' No 1858 is now preserved at the East Anglian Transport Museum at Carlton Colville. Pictured here in August 1972, the tram was then in the process of undergoing long-term restoration.
Michael H. Waller

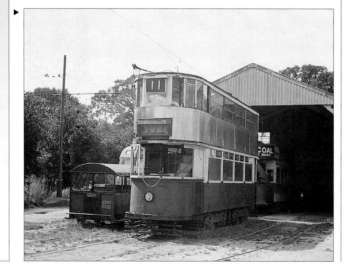

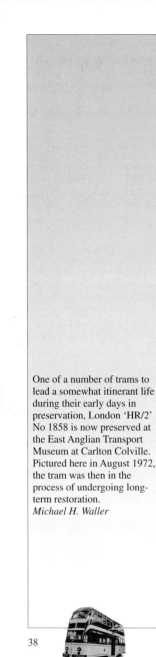

◄ Although tramway preservation started in Great Britain relatively late and numerous fleets had already been abandoned long before Southampton No 45 became the first tram to be secured, representatives of other fleets have been saved after many years of alternative use. Looking deceptively complete in August 1972 Lowestoft No 14 was originally delivered by Milnes in 1904, the year after the system opened. Built to a gauge of 3ft 6in – which is why the tram looks narrow sat on a standard-gauge truck – No 14 survived until the closure of the system on 8 May 1931. After closure, the body was sold off until rescue by the East Anglia Transport Museum Society more than 30 years later. Whilst No 14 survives, it is still, in 2002, a long-term restoration project.
Michael H. Waller

'Goodbye, Old Tram'

▶ By the end of World War 2 the tramcar in the British Isles was undoubtedly endangered and between 1945 and 1962 the number of tramway systems declined from more than 40 possessing more than 5,000 trams to a handful – Blackpool, Douglas, Great Orme, Manx Electric and Snaefell – possessing in total some 200 trams. In many respects the attitude, certainly of those in authority, can be epitomised by Lord Latham's statement – 'Goodbye Old Tram' – at the closure of London's trams in July 1952 and recorded for posterity in the classic film *The Elephant Will Never Forget*. Latham had succeded Lord Ashfield in 1947. The latter had had a pivotal role in the development of public transport in London. Under his control, the Underground group had grown to encompass bus operators Vanguard, Road Car and General as the London General Omnibus Company in 1908 and Ashfield was to play an important role in the continuing amalgamation of public transport in London, culminating in the creation of the London Passenger Transport Board in 1933.

In his statement, Latham perceived the tram as old-fashioned and the LTE was not the only significant provider of public transport to see trolleybuses and motorbuses as providing a better and more modern form of transport. Despite its name, British Electric Traction, one of the country's biggest providers of company-owned public transport, was another pioneer in the development of buses through its subsidiary the Birmingham & Midland Motor Omnibus Company. From these origins in the years before World War 1, the bus developed a capacity able to rival the tram's and, more importantly, it was perceived as being able to provide virtually complete flexibility of operation. In 1903 Eastbourne became the first municipal operators of buses; this was significant because the Corporation had examined, and rejected, the possibility of a municipally-owned tramway. Other non-tramway operators, such as Todmorden, soon appeared and gradually a whole generation of managers came along whose only experience came in the operation of rubber-tyred vehicles.

The role of the individual manager was critical. Whilst the Corporation's Transport Committee might establish policy, in this they were clearly guided by the policy of the General Manager. Thus, Sunderland, a traditional small-town system that might have easily been a victim of the trend towards conversion in the 1930s, survived to be both modernised and extended in the 1940s as a result of the policies of Charles Albert Hopkins, the General

Manager from May 1929 until his death on 16 October 1948 and his successor, H. W. Snowball, who was also pro-tram. Unfortunately the latter's period in control was short, as he died on 1 January 1952, and his successor, Norman Morton, was pro-bus. Thus, almost overnight, Sunderland's position deteriorated and within three years the last trams had been withdrawn. It was rare for a General Manager to be the victim of a policy of which he disapproved; the classic case was probably that of W. G. Marks at Liverpool. Marks was undoubtedly pro-tram; he had overseen the significant development of Liverpool's network during the 1930s, when many routes were extended over segregated reservations and when numerous new trams, most notably the 'Green Goddesses' and 'Baby Grands', were delivered. Marks was honoured to be made President of the LRTL and yet his tramway committee demanded, and got, a policy of tramway abandonment. Forced into this policy, Marks felt honour-bound to resign his position with the LRTL.

By the late 1940s and early 1950s, many of the figures emerging into highest echelons of the industry had cut their teeth with

By 17 June 1962, when this photograph was taken at Dalmuir West, the once great Glasgow tramway system was in its last months. The penultimate route conversion, that of route No 26 from Clydebank to Dalmarnock, had occurred a fortnight earlier, on 2 June 1962, and the last route, No 9, from Dalmuir West to Auchenshuggle would survive only until 4 September. One of the prewar 'Coronation' class, No 1199 is pictured awaiting departure. Built at Coplawhill on EMB Lightweight bogies, 150 trams of this type were constructed between 1936 and 1941. The photograph shows to good effect the section of the road that the tramways had to maintain; under the terms of the 1870 Tramways Act all tramway operators had to maintain the road to a distance of some 18in outside the lines. Although by this date, the rest of this road had also received a proper surface, earlier the unmaintained section of the road could have been little more than mud, thereby forcing other road traffic to use the section constructed for use by trams.

B. G. Tweed/Neville Stead Collection

41

operators that had long since abandoned the use of the tramcar; it was inevitable that they would perceive the tram as old-fashioned and seek to rid themselves of them. In the United States of America, many company-operated tramways had disappeared as a result of the ability of the motor and oil industries to buy shares in the business and effectively engineer closure; in Britain, it was the establishment that often wanted to see the back of the tramcar.

Whilst the tramcar was unpopular to those in authority, it retained, however, its popular appeal. Whilst the authorities might be planning for the tramcar's demise, the local population were often to be found campaigning for its retention. Part of the pro-tram sentiment came from the fact that the replacement bus services were both more unreliable and also more expensive than the trams had been. In 1951, when Sheffield Corporation announced its tramway abandonment policy, an organisation called the Sheffield Tramways Development Association was formed. However, such an organisation was never able to overturn a policy made by the Corporation once the political factions had lined up; in Sheffield, the all-dominant Labour Party had swung from being pro-tram to being anti-tram and, although odd individuals resigned from the party over the policy, once it had become entrenched, it was impossible to reverse.

As befitted a national campaigning society, the Light Railway Transport League produced numerous pamphlets and leaflets arguing strongly for tramway retention and development. In 1951 the LRTL produced a leaflet – *A Solution to Dundee's Transport*

Problems – that sought to provide ammunition for the pro-tram lobby at a time when Dundee was still considering the future of its tramway system. The introduction gave a succinct view of the views of the LRTL at the time:

'League members concern themselves with all forms of transport. It is because the tramcar was found to be superior in many ways, and because this superiority was realised by those concerned only after replacement by bus or trolleybus, that the League was formed to present passengers and local authorities with less of a one-sided picture.'

The leaflet gave a cogent argument in favour of the retention and extension of Dundee's small system concluding:

'The decisions made within the next two year as to the future development of the City's transport system, will, in all probability, determine the mode of transport for a considerable time. No decision will be easily found, no decision will be cheap, thus it is essential that the maximum attention and care be given to any economic proposals, whatever they are and wherever they originate. It would be advisable for our transport management to visit transport undertakings of comparable size to Dundee, both in Great Britain and, particularly, the Continent. For it is in the latter, with their universal use of single-deck trams and trailers, that most can be learnt. Whereas Britain, and

Dundee in particular, was well to the fore in the field of municipal transport, we have now fallen many years behind our contemporaries. It is not outwith the bounds of possibility that, with calculated development, Dundee could once more give an example to the rest of Great Britain.

'The Future is YOUR responsibility.'

In many respects the leaflet was remarkably prescient. The decisions made by the various transport operators in the 1950s did affect the provision of public transport over the next 25 years and, ultimately, it was continental practice that became the norm for investment in the new Light Rail schemes.

As far as Dundee was concerned, the early 1950s did witness a considerable debate about the viability of retention or replacement of the town's small network. However, with only 56 trams and some 12 miles of route many of which were unsuitable for more modern trams due to the alignment of the track, the economic case for retention was difficult.

Despite the difficulties, however, as late as October 1952 the Transport Committee voted to retain the trams and to investigate the possibility of acquiring second-hand trams to replace the city's ageing fleet. However, a number of factors ultimately led to the demise of the trams. the first was the retirement in January 1953 of Robert Taylor, the General Manager of 21 years; as with Snowball and Hopkins in Sunderland, the replacement of a pro-tram manager was detrimental to the network's survival. The second was the

appointment of the former Belfast manager, Robert McCreary, to act as a consultant; McCreary had overseen the introduction of Belfast's tramway conversion policy. The local press reported in March 1953 on his advocacy of tramcar replacement:

'We imagine that only Dundee City Transport Committee is surprised at Colonel R. McCreary's report on its undertaking, in which abandonment of the tramway system is recommended by the end of 1956.... So far Col. McCreary's very commonsense appraisal of the situation appears to have met with nothing but disparaging criticism from members of the Dundee Transport Committee, who still cling to a belief in the rejuvenation of the trams.'

Although the Committee continued to seek a pro-tram solution, the third factor in the ultimate demise of the trams soon came into play – the high cost of new vehicles. It was reported in April 1953 that 'Modern type tramcars are to be sought by Dundee Corporation because some of the existing rolling stock is "a little bit decrepit."'; unfortunately, however, investigation of the possible supply of new trams elicited a price in excess of £20,000 per tram from English Electric leading to the following being reported in June 1953:

'Both Councillors Hardie and Duff, who instituted the inquiry, said that the price was much higher than they had expected.'

Even as late as September 1953 it was reported that the Transport Department was investigating the possibility of the purchase of second-hand trams, probably from Sunderland. However, despite a vigorous pro-tram campaign in the pages of the local press, the trams were ultimately doomed.

Once the final decision to convert was made, the trams could expect to see a final hurrah as the obsequies of closure were marked in a variety of ways. In London, the trams operated with advertisements announcing the 'Last Tram Week' and the fact that the trams were due to say farewell to London on 6 July 1952. The London closure was also marked by the production of special tickets, which pictured on the reverse a horse tram of 1861 and a contemporary electric tram. Huge crowds turned out on the final night of tramway operation, on 5/6 July, and the last trams into New Cross depot, with No 1951 being the last to enter, were mobbed as crowds sang 'Auld Lang Syne' and Lord Ashfield prepared to make his final comments on the demise of the tram. The final days of the London trams were to be graphically recorded in the film *The Elephant Will Never Forget*, which

It's midnight on the night of 20/21 October 1956 and the last east/west tram in Dundee is recorded at Ninewells. Huge crowds turned out to mark the demise of the Dundee system, arguably the last of the country's traditional all-street tramways served by conventional four-wheel cars, with more than 100 travelling on a packed No 45. The tram was officially driven by Ken Watson, although numerous others (including his six-year-old nephew) had a turn. Amongst the passengers on the tram was Bingo, according to the photographer's notes 'the only dog on the last tram'. Along with the locals, who turned out in force to mark the passing of a much loved form of transport, many members of the LRTL also made their way northwards.
Michael H. Waller

By the end of their career, Belfast's tramcars had been effectively restricted to use during the peak hours with all-day services having been withdrawn on 10 October 1953. Gradually over the succeeding months, as 'new' buses (ex-London Transport) entered service, even these remaining peak hour services gradually succumbed so that all tramway operation ceased on 10 February 1954. On 28 February, a final procession was held with 12 cars running from Queens Road to Ardoyne depot with No 389, pictured here, being the last. Although the crowds were out, little had been done to mark the occasion, although one of the advertisers had, unwittingly perhaps, made an ironic comment – the Royal Hippodrome cinema proudly proclaiming 'Farewell the old; Welcome the new.'
Ian Allan Library

Inevitably large crowds were drawn to closure ceremonies and the last trams to operate were regularly popular. This is a view on the lower deck of Aberdeen No 37, one of the postwar Pickering-built bogie cars, on the last day of service, 3 May 1958. The conductor was J. Robertson.
Michael H. Waller

'They draped streamers from every window. On the front, back and sides they hung placards – "Slow but Sure," "The Last Round-up," "Last Stop Harris," "Trams For Ever."

'All the way through the City Centre to Harris Academy they sang and sang. Rowdy maybe, but touching. Enough to bring lumps to the throats of the driver and conductor who had been ploughing the same furrow for three years and knew nearly every kid by name.'

Such unofficial obsequies varied in scale as did the official farewells. Increasingly, during the postwar years, closures came to be marked by processions of trams conveying both invited guests and those locals or enthusiasts able to board them. Sometimes the final trams would be heavily decorated, on other occasions, the

concluded with a comment about how the huge crowds would get home, concluding that 'the next tram had gone'.

Each closure was marked in a slightly different way, but the sense of loss amongst the local population was tangible. By October 1956 the Dundee system was coming towards the end of its life and, for many, this represented a significant change. One of the regular duties performed by the trams was the conveyance home of pupils to and from Harris Academy. Although not part of any formal closure celebrations, the pupils bedecked the last tram to convey them to school on the morning of 19 October with ribbons and hand-written slogans. The event was recorded on the front page of that evening's *Evening Telegraph and Post*. Alongside a photograph of a packed No 30 was a report:

'TA-TA TO THE HARRIS TRAM
'Lochee tram terminus, 8.27 a.m.

'From the screaming and shouting, the flash of maroon, you could tell it was the Harris Academy special.

'The 85 school kids who choked the doors, platforms and stairs made sure everyone would know it!

last tram was just the final service car with nothing to indicate that on the following day its next journey may well be to the scrapyard. Sheffield, for example, repainted two of the Roberts-built trams, Nos 510 and 513, in October 1960 with panels depicting scenes from tramway history in the city. Inevitably the local media would cover the event. The Dundee *Courier & Advertiser* reported in graphic detail the events of 20 October 1956 when the city's last tramcar ran:

'I have never seen anything like it. Hundreds of cars lining the streets, thousands of people milling around, cheering, waving and singing, fireworks lighting the scene – and all in the wee sma' hours of a Sunday morning.
'The reason for all this was the last tram run from Maryfield to Lochee, ending an era for Dundee's Transport Department.
'When I arrived at Maryfield depot about midnight on

Saturday for my last tram trip I expected a few diehards waiting to see the fun. I could hardly believe my eyes.
'The street was filled, and people stood at windows to pay their respects...
'The earlier scenes were nothing to those in the City Centre. The track was lined ten deep by folk waving and cheering.'

Amongst the 'joy' however, there was much sadness again as recorded by the *Courier* reporter:

'As a special bus drove away with the official party I looked round the now silent depot. The familiar green and white vehicles waited, as it were, with a calm and detached air.
'Today they go on the back of a lorry to the breakers' yard. The city streets will be quieter, but I will never forget the night I saw an old friend go down.'

A Bright Tomorrow?

Britain's rush to abandon its tramways both during the 1930s and then after World War 2 was not unique. Other European countries, such as Denmark, Italy and France, also witnessed the elimination of most, if not all, of their traditional tramway networks. Elsewhere, however, tramways continued to operate, often being perceived as the precursors of more advanced (and expensive) metro systems. In Britain, the all-conquering internal combustion engine came to dominate and it was not until the last quarter of the 20th century that the exponents of tramway – or Light Rapid Transit – systems were, once again, to find favour. The pioneering second-generation system, however, owed more to heavy rail than to more conventional tramways. The Tyne & Wear Metro had the benefit of a suburban railway network, previously electrified (by the North Eastern Railway), onto which new underground sections through central Newcastle and a new crossing of the Tyne could be added.

Undoubtedly one advantage that the Tyne & Wear Metro possessed in its development was that it was not planned as an on-street operation. It was able to take advantage of existing railway infrastructure which was either transferred to enable conversion completely or, on certain sections (most notably over the route to Kenton Bankfoot), alongside extant railway services. Although the underground sections through Newcastle and Gateshead did cause some disruption, its development was perceived as being a modernisation of an existing railway. More recent developments of the Tyne & Wear Metro, most notably the £100 million extension through Sunderland to South Hylton, which opened in 2002, have pursued the same policy, running along the existing line to Sunderland and then over a previously closed branch. However, although early days, it would appear that the returns from this extension are not as great as anticipated and have proved to be a financial drain.

If the Tyne & Wear Metro sought to build upon and extend the existing use of a suburban railway network, the next major development was to be an exercise in social engineering and urban renewal. With the rise of container traffic, the traditional port of London was in terminal decline, leaving vast tracts of land derelict. The potential for commercial redevelopment was there, but the public transport infrastructure was not. The Docklands Light Railway was designed to provide that infrastructure. Officially opened by the Queen on 30 July 1987, the routes provided connections between Tower Gateway – soon to be extended underground to make a connection with the London Underground network at Bank – Stratford and Island Gardens.

Looking undoubtedly more like a railway than a tramway, the formation of the Midland Metro stretches into the distance at Wednesbury on 3 May 1998. *Peter Waller*

Undoubtedly the provision of the network was a factor in the renewal of this otherwise depressed area, but it would be a mistake to see DLR as being a complete success from the start. Teething problems with the computers and automatic trains often caused failures in service, with the trains often having to be placed in manual mode. However, with the problems eventually ironed out the system has proved capable of handling the large numbers using it daily. Further extensions have seen the DLR extended to Beckton, north of the Thames, and to Lewisham via Greenwich. Further expansion is planned, including a link to the London City Airport.

The one common factor between Tyne & Wear and the DLR was that neither involved on-street running. That was to change with the promotion of Manchester Metrolink. Manchester possessed two major station – Victoria and Piccadilly – but there was no direct rail connection between the two and, for many years, there had been plans for improved public transport connections between the two, including the proposed Picc-Vic underground line. As matters stood, however, the only connection was provided by minibuses running at frequent intervals through the city centre. Sponsored by the Greater Manchester PTE, Manchester Metrolink was designed to take over two conventional railway routes – to Bury in the north and Altrincham in the south – and link them via a street section with Piccadilly station. The ambitious scheme was opened in 1992 and has subsequently been extended to Eccles; both the city centre section and the route to Eccles possess stretches of street running. The success of the Metrolink scheme has resulted in further extensions being proposed, including the conversion of the existing railway line to Rochdale via Oldham with a deviation in Oldham to serve the town centre and an extension at the northern end into Rochdale centre. However, current proposals for this extension and that southwards to serve Manchester airport are estimated to cost some £200 million and require the purchase of some 400 properties.

The next LRT scheme to come to fruition in the UK was that serving South Yorkshire – the Sheffield Supertram. Approved in December 1990, the Supertram network comprises some 30km in length, running east to west through the city and providing links to the suburbs, much of which is constructed for on-street running, with a link northwards to serve the huge shopping complex at Meadowhall. The northern section was largely constructed on former railway alignments. Although the Supertram's figures were initially disappointing, they have improved over recent years and, as with Manchester, there are ambitious proposals for further extensions.

Long in gestation, the Midland Metro, between Birmingham and Wolverhampton, finally opened in 1999. Largely constructed on the trackbed of the ex-Great Western main line between Birmingham Snow Hill and Wolverhampton Low Level, the route deviates at the western end to run, via a street section, into Wolverhampton town centre. Again there are ambitious plans for the further development of the network, with the moribund railway line between Stourbridge and Walsall being considered as the next phase allied to a connection with the Merryhill Shopping Centre.

The most recent scheme to open is that serving Croydon, which brought street trams back to the London for the first time in almost 50 years. The bulk of the network, as elsewhere, features the use of converted railway lines, most notably from Wimbledon to Croydon and from Addiscombe to Elmers End, but the most impressive street-running section provides a loop through central Croydon linking West Croydon and East Croydon stations with the central shopping and business area. Equally impressive is the route constructed to serve New Addington. Such has been the success of Croydon Tramlink that it has encouraged plans both for its own extension but also, and perhaps more significantly, the construction of LRT schemes to serve Central London in order to alleviate the over-stretched London Underground. If plans come to fruition a new tramway running from Brixton to Camden via Holborn and Russell Square, for example, will be in operation within a decade.

At the time of writing, Britain's next LRT scheme is well advanced: Nottingham Express Transit is currently under

One of the major concerns raised by opponents of modern LRT schemes is the potential disruption caused to road traffic during construction. In the early 1950s, everything was so much more straightforward as demonstrated by this view of relaying work in progress at Downfield, Dundee, on 12 April 1952. In the distance can be seen car No 13, one of a batch of eight trams delivered from Milnes in 1902 which were rebuilt as fully-enclosed between 1928 and 1930. Further away can be seen a solitary car; the absence of all the protective paraphernalia of the 21st century is also conspicuous. *Michael H. Waller*

Undoubtedly one factor that has led to opposition to the promotion of new LRT schemes in Britain has been the fear of disruption caused by the actual construction process and by a belief that this would result is loss of business. This opposition has been particularly strong in Croydon and in Nottingham. This scene in Croydon, pictured early in 1999, shows the potential scale of the engineering works associated with the construction process. *Peter Waller*

construction. This will provide a link from the city's railway station, through the city centre, to the northern suburbs. Within central Nottingham itself there will be street running, whilst to the north of the city the first line will effectively parallel the recently restored passenger service towards Bulwell. Further schemes, such as that serving Leeds, are under active development. However, cost is a problem. Proposals for the construction of a single route in Liverpool, from the Mersey to Kirkby, are estimated at £150 million, for example, and a number of consultants are now arguing that other schemes, such as guided busways (like that recently introduced onto Manchester Road in Bradford), offer a more cost-effective solution.

Thus at the start of the 21st century it may well be that we're entering the second period of 'Glory Days' for Britain's trams. If we are, then the jury is probably still out for a number of reasons. Firstly, the huge cost of many of these proposals is such that the question of funding becomes critical. Large projects can only be funded with the support of central government, an institution that has proved itself unwilling or unable to commit to more than a limited number of projects. Moreover as the existing systems seek additional funding to expand so new schemes may find it difficult to gain approval.

A second problem arises from the competitive nature of modern public transport provision. As a result of privatisation and deregulation, the whole ethos of integration that made Tyne & Wear, for example, highly successful through the operation of feeder bus routes, has disappeared. Instead, there are no barriers to prevent competition between LRT operators and existing local bus companies; this competition is both wasteful and also likely to make marginal schemes more unlikely to obtain funding.

Thirdly, as shown at Croydon, there is still an unwillingness amongst some to accept short-term hardship for the undoubted benefit that a modern LRT scheme can bring. Croydon Tramlink carried 18.2 million passengers in 2001/02, exactly the same as carried by Manchester Metrolink, out a total in the UK of 127.3 million. However, proposals by the Mayor of London, Ken Livingstone, to restore trams to the Shepherds Bush-Ealing corridor has met with a 10,000 name petition opposing any work on the basis of the disruption likely to be caused.

With congestion charging coming to London in February 2003, and with similar schemes being proposed for other major cities, LRT *should* have an important role in public transport provision. It may well be that there is a new 'Golden Age' around the corner; there's no way of knowing, however, whether we are approaching it or whether the current LRT schemes represent a false dawn.

Pictured at the Bridge of Don terminus of Aberdeen's main north-south route is No 48. This was one of 14 trams acquired second-hand from Manchester in 1948 and was numbered 270 in the Manchester fleet. Known as 'Pilcher' cars after the then Manchester manager, Stuart Pilcher, these cars, built originally between 1930 and 1932 were the last new trams to be delivered to Manchester. Unfortunately, efforts to try and secure one of the 'Pilcher' cars for preservation after their withdrawal from Aberdeen in 1955/56 came to nothing.
J. Copland/Photobus

Aberdeen No 107, again pictured on route No 1 between Bridge of Don and Bridge of Dee, was delivered new to the corporation in 1925, the first of a batch of eight built by Brush on Peckham P35 trucks. The Bridges route was destined to be the last Aberdeen tram service, being converted to bus operation on 3 May 1958.
J. Copland/Photobus

In the immediate post-World War 2 years, Scotland possessed four tramway systems. At the time all four were considered to be as secure as any other in the country. At the LRTL AGM in 1949, the Scottish Liaison Officer, the author's late father, reported: 'Aberdeen presents a very healthy picture, as we have witnessed the arrival of twenty new streamline tramcars from Messrs. R. Y. Pickerings [sic].... The Woodside route is to be completely relaid, and work is in hand at the moment. There is hope that the construction of the new route to Sea Beach may recommence at an early date'. Undoubtedly such optimism was justified but, with the benefit of hindsight, proved wrong. The 20 trams delivered in 1949, Nos 19-38, were destined to have a working life of less than a decade, being withdrawn when the system closed in 1958. One of the 20, No 29, is pictured at Bridge of Don.
J. Copland/Photobus

Whilst it may have been obvious for seaside resorts like Blackpool to offer specific services for tourists, other towns and cities also felt that they could cater for the traveller or tourist. Although this wartime guide for Aberdeen features primarily coach tours operated by the Corporation, it also advertised a 'Shilling All-Day Ticket' allowing unlimited travel by Corporation tram or bus. The wartime conditions, however, forced the inclusion of the following statement: 'WAR EMERGENCY NOTICE – Wherever reference is made to the BEACH in any of the tours in this Booklet the CORPORATION OF ABERDEEN desires to inform passengers that a certain part of the BEACH is closed to Vehicular Traffic. Tours in that direction are therefore slightly curtailed'. *Author's Collection*

One of the 50 'Chamberlain' cars supplied to Belfast in 1930, No 374, is seen emerging from Station Street and on to Bridge End. If the Mountpottinger destination is correct, the car will be about to turn to its left. Of the 50 cars in the class, 40, including No 374, were built by Brush and the remainder by Service Motor Co in Belfast.
W.E. Robertson/Colour-Rail (IR472)

No 342 was the prototype of the 'Chamberlain' type in Belfast and was supplied by Brush in 1930. The cars were fitted with Maley & Taunton swing-link trucks and, at 33ft in length, were the longest trams to operate in the city. The tram is pictured here entering what was known as the tram dock at Queen's Quay, Belfast & County Down Railway, station via an entrance on Scrabo Street. The destination was shown as 'Co Down Railway' on destination blinds. This was one of two termini in Belfast located in railway stations; the other was at the Northern Counties Committee station at York Road. This arrangement was probably unique to Belfast; indeed, apart from the recent Manchester Metrolink service through Manchester Victoria and under Manchester Piccadilly, it is impossible to think of any other system in the British Isles which took integration as far as in Belfast.
W.E. Robertson/Colour-Rail (IR339)

The last new trams delivered
to Belfast were the 50
'McCreary' or 'Streamliner'
cars introduced in 1935.
Twenty-five of the type,
Nos 392 and 418-41, were
built by English Electric and
the remainder by Service
Motor Co on Hurst Nelson
underframes. The cars were
32ft in length and provided
seats for 64 passengers. The
main distinguishing feature
between the Belfast-built
examples, such as No 397
pictured at the Ligoneil
terminus, and the Preston-
built batch was that the
latter's headlamp was set at a
slightly higher level.
*W.E. Robertson/Colour-Rail
(IR413)*

In 1924-25, Brush supplied 40 cars, Nos 662-701, to Birmingham Corporation; of these the majority survived World War 2, but seven were destroyed in 1941 during an air raid. One of those to survive the war, No 668, is seen at Short Heath terminus in the spring of 1953. The route to Short Heath, an extension from Stockland Road, opened on 23 June 1926, was one of the last extensions to be opened in the city. The Short Heath service, built to serve a new housing estate, was to be one of the last Birmingham routes to survive, being converted to bus operation on 4 July 1953. *I. Davidson/Colour-Rail (IR346)*

The Blackpool 'Standards' represented the last of the traditional British four-wheel trams to remain in service when the last examples were withdrawn in the mid-1960s. Almost two decades earlier No 152 looks in fine condition on 19 May 1950 at Royal Oak. *C. Carter*

Pictured in Manchester Square, Blackpool, in June 1975 is Brush-built railcoach No 631 with, in the background, one of the double-deck 'Balloon' cars and one of the One-Man rebuilds. No 631 was one of the 20 cars, Nos 284-303, delivered in 1937. In 1968, the remaining 18 of the batch (Nos 284-300 and 302) were renumbered 621-38. Of these, a number have now been withdrawn (including No 635 which is preserved), although the majority remain in service. These were the last trams to be manufactured by Brush; although, thereotically, the company retained a capacity to build trams thereafter, no orders were forthcoming. *Michael H. Waller*

57

Between 1972 and 1976, Blackpool rebuilt 13 of the English Electric railcoaches at Rigby Road for One-Man Operation. Numbered 1-13, the rebuilt trams were originally painted in the red/yellow livery carried here by No 5, seen at Starr Gate in June 1975. No 5 was originally railcoach No 220 (which should have carried the number 608 from 1968 but was in fact never renumbered) and was rebuilt in 1972. All 13 of the One-Man cars have now been withdrawn from service, a process commencing in 1984.
Michael H. Waller

The horse tramway of Douglas, in the Isle of Man, is now well into its second century, having been opened initially in 1876. Here toastrack No 33, one of six (Nos 32-7) delivered by Milnes in 1896, makes its stately progress towards the northern terminus at Douglas Castle on 18 September 2000.
Peter Waller

On 16 July 1955 Dundee No 47 heads eastbound along Perth Road with a service to Maryfield via the High Street. No 47 was one of a batch of cars delivered from Hurst Nelson in 1916 and had been originally numbered 77 (and renumbered 73 in 1927). Constructed when new with open balconies but with enclosed top decks, the car had been rebuilt as fully enclosed in 1932 at which time the original EMB flexible truck had been replaced with a Brill 21E.
Chris Banks Collection/ Colour-Rail

Looking eastwards towards the Clydesdale Bank building at the end of the High Street, two trams head towards the junction between the Downfield and Maryfield routes. No 31, nearest to the camera, was one of a batch of fully-enclosed trams built in Dundee's own workshops in the mid-1920s; delivered in 1926 as No 96, the car was renumbered 83 before being finally renumbered 31 in 1936. The car was fitted with a Peckham P35 truck from new. *Chris Banks Collection/ Colour-Rail (IR227)*

Edinburgh No 186 was one of a number of fully-enclosed cars delivered in the early 1930s following construction in the Corporation's own Shrubhill Works. The cars were fitted with Peckham P22 trucks and were fitted with top covers salvaged from the earlier trams of the same number. *J. Copland/Photobus*

Edinburgh No 214, seen here on route 11 to Stanley Road was typical of the trams constructed in Edinburgh's own Shrubhill Works on Peckham P22 trucks between 1934 and 1950. Sister car No 35 was eventually to be preserved, the only electric car to survive from the Edinburgh system. *J. Copland/Photobus*

The 'electrified magnet' of the BET Group was a familiar symbol associated with trams in the country for some 50 years but, by 1945, BET's interests in tramways had declined inexorably. Its last town system was represented by that of Gateshead. As a result of a number of low bridges within the town, Gateshead & District operated a large fleet of single-deck trams alongside its own double-deckers as well as those of Newcastle Corporation on the joint services across the River Tyne. No 1, one of 20 single deckers built by Brush between 1920 and 1928, is pictured at Newcastle Central station on 16 February 1949. After withdrawal, 19 Gateshead trams, including No 1, were sold for use on the Grimsby & Immingham line, although only 17 entered passenger service (an 18th was used as a works car and a 19th, ex-Gateshead No 4, was destroyed in transit). Of these, two, Nos 5 and 10, have been preserved. *C. Carter*

Pictured towards the end of its working life, Glasgow 'Standard' No 72 was originally built in August 1920 as an open-balcony top-cover car and was to receive enclosed balconies in February 1929. During their long careers, with construction continuing for some two decades and rebuilding over some 60 years, the Glasgow 'Standard' numbered more than 1,000 examples and evolved from being open-topped and open-vestibuled to the majority being fully enclosed. Although the Blackpool 'Balloons' can now claim to be as long-lived, the Glasgow 'Standards' were perhaps the last traditional British double-deck tram to be seen in significant numbers. No 72 was withdrawn in October 1960, some two years before the withdrawal of Glasgow's final route.
J. Copland/Photobus

Although bearing a relatively low fleet number, No 11 was in fact one of the last of the Glasgow 'Standard' cars to be produced, being completed in July 1923. By the early 1950s, the Glasgow 'Standard' cars represented the single biggest class of traditional British tram still in service. It is seen on route No 31, between Lambhill and Merrylee, a service that was converted to bus operation on 5 December 1959, although No 11 was not to survive until that route's closure, being withdrawn in February of the same year.
J. Copland/Photobus

◄◄ Known unofficially as 'Kilmarnock Bogies', 52 trams of this type were delivered to Glasgow Corporation between 1927 and 1929. The first two – Nos 140 and 1090 (both fitted with Hurst Nelson maximum-traction bogies) – were constructed at the corporation's own Coplawhill Works. The remainder, starting with No 1091 illustrated here, were built by outside contractors: Nos 1091-1120 by Hurst Nelson, Nos 1121-30 by Pickering, and Nos 1131-40 by Brush. All those bought from outside manufacturers were fitted with maximum-traction bogies supplied by the Kilmarnock Engineering Co. Two of the type, Nos 1100 (as rebuilt in 1941) and 1115, survive in preservation at the National Tramway Museum.
J. Copland/Photobus

◄ During the four years between March 1937 and July 1941, Glasgow constructed 150 'Coronation' class cars in its workshops at Coplawhill. No 1187, seen here on route No 29 heading towards Tollcross, was new in June 1938 and was to survive in service until June 1962. By that date, the Tollcross service was no more, having been converted to bus operation on 21 October 1961.
J. Copland/Photobus

In April 1975 the two lower-section cars on the Great Orme tramway pass at the mid-point of the route. Nos 4 and 5 were built by Hurst Nelson and delivered in 1902. *Peter Johnson*

One of the Great Central cars built for the Grimsby & Immingham, No 11, is pictured at the Grimsby Corporation Bridge terminus. The section from Corporation Bridge to Cleveland Bridge was the first section of the line to close with services being withdrawn on 30 June 1956. No 11 was one of four cars, Nos 9-12, delivered from Brush in 1913. After Nationalisation in 1948, the line's fleet of trams was painted in the standard all-over green livery applied by British Railways to EMUs. *Ian Davidson/Colour-Rail (DE1616)*

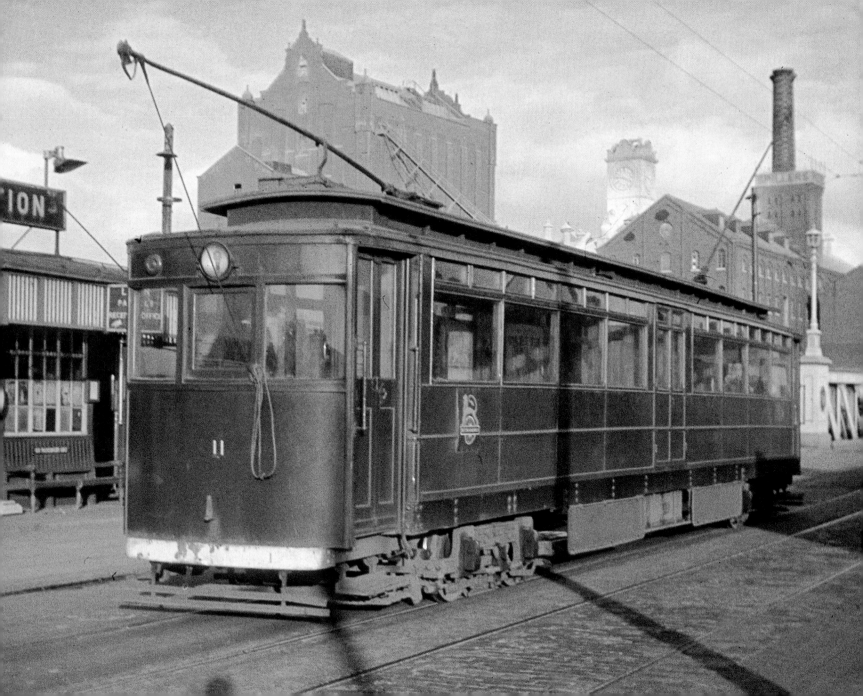

Hill of Howth No 4 was one of the eight cars delivered to the line by Brush for the line's opening in 1901. It is seen on 2 October 1953. After withdrawal, No 4 was one of the line's trams to be preserved and is now on display in Belfast.
Colour-Rail

During 1931 and 1932, Brush constructed 100 four-wheel cars following on from four prototypes, Nos 151-4, constructed in Leeds' own workshops at Kirkstall. Numbered 155-254, the 'Horsfelds', nicknamed after the manager (R. L. Horsfeld) who had desgned the prototypes and who had died in 1931 (aged only 57) whilst the first of the new cars was being delivered, were offically known as 'P35s' or 'Showboats'. No 199, delivered in July 1931, was destined to have a working life of more than a quarter of a century. It is seen on route No 3 to Roundhay, a service that was converted to bus operaton on 28 March 1959.
J. Copland/Photobus

Nicknamed 'Lance
Corporals' for obvious
reasons, Leeds No 272 was
the first of a batch of three
delivered to the corporation
from its own Kirkstall Lane
Works in 1935. Fitted wth
Maley & Taunton Swing Link
bogies, the three cars were to
remain in service until 1955.
J. Copland/Photobus

The 17 'Middleton Bogies',
Nos 255-271, were delivered
to Leeds from two
manufacturers between 1933
and 1935. No 255 (the
prototype) and Nos 256-63
came from Brush whilst the
rest came from English
Electric, although all were
fitted wth Maley & Taunton
bogies. One the Brush-built
vehicles, No 257, heads
eastwards on route No 20 to
Halton. The Halton route,
renumbered from No 17 in
1945, was one of the last
Leeds routes to be converted,
succumbing with the rest of
the York Road services on
7 November 1959. By that
date, however, the 'Middleton
Bogies' were themselves
history, being withdrawn in
1956/57. It is a shame that
none of these stylish trams was
to survive into preservation.
J. Copland/Photobus

Liverpool No 765 was one of 12 cars, Nos 758-69, produced in the Corporation's own workshops and delivered in 1931/32. Originally fitted with English Electric equal wheel bogies, No 765 was one of those subsequently fitted with EMB Lightweight bogies between 1937 and 1944. The car is seen on route No 40, to Page Moss, which was destined to be one of the last two routes in Liverpool, converted on 14 September 1957. Although none of the type were preserved, the lower-deck from No 762 was preserved in 1977 after passing to the Parks Department on withdrawal. *J. B. McCann/Colour-Rail (IR432)*

Two of Liverpool's 'Baby Grands', Nos 235 and 266, pass on James Street whilst operating on routes 40 and 6A respectively on 19 April 1957. By this date the Liverpool system had been reduced to these two routes alone and had barely five months to go before final abandonment. Despite this, both cars, the products of Liverpool's own workshops in the late 1930s, look in good condition. Between the trams and the offices can be seen another part of Liverpool transport heritage – the bridge carrying the much-mourned Liverpool Overhead Railway. *Colour-Rail*

The last 3ft 6in gauge tramway to operate on the mainland was the Llandudno & Colwyn Bay Electric Railway and, when the line was threatened with closure in the mid-1950s, efforts were made to preserve it. Unfortunately, these plans failed and the line closed on 24 March 1956. For many years, the mainstay of the line's fleet was represented by 10 open-top cars acquired from Bournemouth in 1936, the oldest of which was No 6, pictured here. This car was originally Bournemouth No 85 and delivered from the United Electric Car Co Ltd in 1914. On withdrawal, this car was preserved and displayed for a period at the Clapham Museum of Transport. Subsequently returned to Bournemouth, it was restored to its original condition.
J. B. McCann/Colour-Rail (IR434)

The L&CBER was a user, like Blackpool, of toastrack trams and was the last line to operate such cars on the mainland in regular public service. Four open toastrack cars were built by English Electric and delivered to the line in 1920. One of the quartet, No 21, is pictured heading eastbound towards Colwyn Bay. All four were withdrawn at the end of the summer season in 1955.
T. J. Edgington/Colour-Rail (IR168)

Pictured at New Cross on 13 August 1950 is this trio of London trams with 'E1' class No 1614 nearest to the camera. The three cars were stationary as a result of a crew-change where no replacement crew was available. Towards the end of London's trams this became an increasing problem and resulted in the trams receiving a bad name. *C. Carter*

Laxey is the point at which the 3ft 0in gauge Manx Electric Railway meets the 3ft 6in gauge Snaefell Mountain Railway and is, therefore, one of the busiest intermediate stations on the line, particularly in good weather during the holiday season. Here Snaefell No 4 awaits its next departure whilst passengers board an MER service towards Douglas. Power car No 28 was one of four crossbench cars delivered in 1904 from UEC. *J. Copland/Photobus*

Laxey remains the focal point of the MER/SMR in the 21st century, even though the passenger figures may not be as great as they were in the halcyon days of the British seaside holiday. Here, on 19 September 2000, a southbound service heads into Laxey. The two-car rake is formed of winter saloon No 19, delivered in 1899 from Milnes, with crossbench trailer No 42, again supplied by Milnes, but this time in 1903. *Peter Waller*

79

Newcastle, like a number of other systems, had introduced a wholesale tramway conversion programme in the 1930s and by the outbreak of war, much of the 50-route mile network had succumbed. Wartime exigencies, however, meant the system was give a short-term reprieve, although the process of conversion started again in June 1946. The last new Newcastle trams had been delivered in 1926 and the fleet towards the end of its life looked increasingly out-of-date compared with the new trolleybuses and motorbuses replacing them. No 197, illustrated here at Central station on 13 September 1949, was one of 37 Class E cars manufactured by the Corporation itself and by Brush between 1912 and 1918. The final Newcastle tram operated on 4 March 1950, although the streets of Newcastle were to resound with the sound of metal on metal for a further year as Gateshead continued to operate across the Tyne. *C. Carter*

The clean lines of the production batch of Roberts-built trams are evident in this photograph of Sheffield No 521 taken on the loop at Millhouses. The 35 cars built by Roberts between 1950 and 1952, Nos 502-36, represented the last new trams acquired by Sheffield and followed the basic design established in the prototype car, No 501, built by the Corporation in 1946. Amongst the differences were the use of steel framing rather than composite construction and the position of the sidelights. Fitted with Maley & Taunton trucks, the 'Roberts' cars survived until the end of the Sheffield system.
J. Copland/Photobus

Also pictured at the Millhouses loop is Sheffield No 194, one of batch of 45 cars constructed in the Corporation's own workshops in 1933/34 on Peckham P22 trucks. Two of this batch, Nos 192 and 201, were destroyed during World War 2 whilst a third, No 189, is now preserved at the National Tramway Museum. The loop at Millhouses was opened in 1927 and was to survive until removal in August 1960, a few months before the final withdrawal of Sheffield's trams on 8 October 1960. The loop was provided with a passenger shelter, visible to the right, which has clearly been put to good use as passengers board the tram. *J. Copland/Photobus*

There's clearly plenty of room on top as passengers patiently wait to board Sheffield No 72 en route to Woodseats. The front seats on the top deck have, however, already been taken. No 72 was originally built in Sheffield's own workshops as one of a batch of 70, Nos 61-130, built between 1930 and 1933 on Peckham P22 trucks. However, a number of the class, including No 72, were rebuilt between 1952 and 1956 with modified lower decks. No 72 was one of the last of its type to survive in service, not being withdrawn until early August 1960. *J. Copland/Photobus*

Pictured at Laxey are two of the six cars that form the fleet operated by the Snaefell Mountain Railway. Closest to the camera is No 4 in the green and white livery that was briefly adopted in the late 1950s whilst No 5 alongside is in the more regular livery. The body of No 5 was to be destroyed in a fire and replaced by a replica constructed in 1971.
J. Copland/Photobus

More than a century after its opening, the Snaefell Mountain Railway continues to fulfil the aims of the promoters of the route at the end of the 19th century: the safe conveyance of visitors to the top of the 2,100ft high peak. With the Manx landscape forming a backdrop, No 1 can be seen ascending towards the summit on 22 September 2000. Clearly visible are the twin fixed bow collectors that provide the power to the cars. These were patented by John Hopkinson, who supervised the installation of the line's electricity supply, and for a time similar collectors were fitted to the trams used on the associated Manx Electric Railway. *Peter Waller*

Nicknamed the 'Ghost Tram' as a result of its quiet operation and the secrecy under which it was built, No 86 was constructed by Sunderland Corporation in its own workshops at Hylton Road in 1932 on an EMB Hornless truck. Pictured on the Seaburn via Fulwell route, No 86 was destined to become Sunderland's official last tram. *J. Copland/Photobus*

Between 1938 and 1940, Sunderland constructed four streamlined trams, Nos 49-52, at Hylton Road to the design of English Electric using English Electric built trucks. One of the batch is pictured at the Seaburn terminus of the route via Roker towards the end of its life. Of the quartet, two (Nos 50 and 51) were withdrawn in June 1953 and the remaining two in January 1954. *J. Copland/Photobus*

South Yorkshire Supertram No 121 heads for Meadowhall on 28 August 2002 crossing the system's distinctive bow-arch bridge. The tram is painted in the familiar livery of Stagecoach, as this company now holds the concession for the system's operation. *Brian Morrison*

Pictured running on the trackbed of the former Great Western Railway main line, Midland Metro trams Nos 12 and 05 cross with services to Wolverhampton St George's and Birmingham Snow Hill respectively at Black Lake. *Alistair Grieve*